House of Women

House of Women

Mary.

There is power in
a House of Women
May you find joy
with this sharing

Peace & blessings

Given to you

Mitchell

Gwendolyn A. Mitchell

Third World Press, Chicago

Third World Press, Publishers Since 1967
© 2002 by Gwendolyn A. Mitchell

Printed in the United States of America

05 04 03 02   5 4 3 2 1

Cover art and design by Nicole M. Mitchell
Author photo by Walter S. Mitchell III

Library of Congress Cataloging-in-Publication Data

Mitchell, Gwendolyn A. (Gwendolyn Ann), 1955-
    House of women / Gwendolyn A. Mitchell
        p. cm.
ISBN 0-88378-222-7 (alk.paper) ISBN 0-88378-223-5(pbk.:alk.paper)
    1. Afro-American women--Poetry I.Title.

PS3563.I763 H68 2002
811'.6--dc21

                                                  00-037760

For my Mother and Father

Acknowledgments

Grateful acknowledgment is made to the editors and publishers of the following publications, where some of the poems in this collection first appeared: *Veins and Rivers*; *The American Voice*; *Prairie Schooner*; *Warpland: A Journal of Black Literature and Ideas*; *Lines and Ribbons Anthology*; *Kalliope: The Pennsylvania State University Literary Magazine*; *5 A.M., Pittsburgh*; *Women and Death*. Many of the poems in this collection were originally published in *Loud in the Heat Streets*.

The production of *House of Women* was made possible, in part, by a grant from the Commonwealth of Pennsylvania Council on the Arts.

Contents

House of Women

I come from a house of women
so no one ever told me that I should not,
if I could, why not?
Girl, you do it.
Sing if you want to but
Where did you get that song?

Mommas, Babies, and short'n bread chant
from the second-level piano music book
with a fill-in-the-color picture of girls
their hair in short bowed plaits
and a round aproned-woman.
My mother never made
shortening bread
and she would tell me
the word has a "g" on the end,
I want to hear you say it when you sing.

But sing if you want to
or write your own fair tale of ever after
once or twice upon a clock is ticking.
The moment is marked in volumes above shout.
We can all shout and joyful noise make with ease,
it is our blood,
blues on the inside,
hide your soul and sing
the night chorus.

How strong you look by moon,
how gentle the talk, like whisper.
Watch wait
you rehearse the woman sounds,
the voice is hushed to tears,
by morning is seen a woman working,
she knows the source of sacred song.

Notes on Womanhood
(The Breast Poem)

I don't hide anymore,
letting my breasts air
after milking.
        But
at thirteen, I snuck
my sister's brassiere
into the bathroom,
tucked rolled stockings
under my cardigan and prayed
the mirror wouldn't give up secrets.
But too embarrassed to reveal
that new-found fullness,
I left for school
flat-chested as ever.
That's when the breasts became sacred.

So when I read about the girl
and her waiting horror—
"Those awful hanging breasts"—
I knew the reason she could
not turn away, why fascination
kept her staring, wanting to touch them,
jealous of those women
who could be so free.
She was horrified of what would become
of her own smooth flesh.

I'd almost forgotten
my longing to be grown
until today, holding my child,
watching his open mouth
search for the comfort of my dark
nipple. He latches on.
For him it's a matter of life.

Prodigal Spirit

I was the prodigal spirit waiting for embrace
waiting for the call to comfort
stay now, stay in the bosom of all that is holy and home.
The ethereal spirit hovering above the ancestral gathering
waiting to enter the body of creation.

Why are they staring as if they can not see me?
Am I the sift of snow that blurs,
a single flake holding definition only in air?
I've been too long gone
and have lost my way, I can't get back,
can't get back to the place or the memory of the place.
What street, what corner, what did I call myself then,
those times, when I would answer?

Extravagant pleasures of earth
overwhelmed, wanting all filled my days and nights.
I, the beautiful dreams, gave life to each desire.
This abundance was not strange to any one that saw
but envied until it ceased to be
and I ceased to belong even to myself.

I took the lowly place,
becoming no more than the street beggar
seated on the city walk
in the shadow of my father's sight.
But he caught full vision,

This is my child returned, he cried.

My wasteful, foolish spirit
welcomed as if unchanged,
grounded once again in earth's footing.

Bring Something of Yourself and
Leave it There

Watch her, remember her movement
watch her, she is trying to show you something
and you so afraid that it might require something of you.

She asks me to rub her legs
"Don't be afraid to rub them hard."
"It feels like something's eating me up," she says. "Do
you see anything?
God help me."
So I rub her legs. Take the lotion from her bag
and massage the
ninety-plus-year-old skin
　　　　legs that no longer bear the weight of her body,
　　　　　　　tender feet propped and pillowed
"That's better," she says. "I'm all right now."

What did she do all those years
before this place confined her life—resident on the third
floor east wing
sitting in the solarium?
Woman in this room of mostly women
taken from the routine of summer gardens
and Sunday dinners,
knowing she'll never leave this place
so she don't ask no more about going home
and he's been gone almost five years.

"Seems I just got tired," she says, "time for someone to
do for me for a change."

Remnants of a former life
        spill out in casual conversation.
That was my advertisement in the daily paper

> LAUNDRESS wants family wash,
> do at my home. Experienced
> men's shirts, children's clothes. PE 1-6576.

Had three calls the first day
Would allow them to come in through my front door
        wait in the foyer
            until my niece came calling
                "Some white women here to see
                you, Aunt Ora."
I like to see their reaction—I had an elegant
hill side home—just because I
kept houses don't mean I don't
know how to keep my own
Victorian lace and polished cherry wood.

"Have a seat, won't you please."
I watch the women carefully sit stiffly on the
edge of my couch.

How she live like we do, they must be thinking.
I watch them watching me from behind the polite smile

didn't know what to expect inside a colored
woman's home.

> I have a three day turn-around
> or you can drop off and pick up the same
> day each week.
> I don't do weekends.
> Latest pick up is six o'clock.
> I do light mending—for a fee.
> Please presort.
> Pleats and spotting are extra.
> Have items delivered to my side door.
> Here are my references.
> My rates are reasonable and
> not negotiable.

I tell them, you see, I just did this part time
wanted to stay busy in my middle age
idle hands devil's workshop,
invite them for tea and homemade
melt-in-your-mouth
butter cookies or pound cake.

> know they be thinking
> maybe I'll do some holiday baking on the side.

Washing some one's filth and grime is
an intimacy you don't dare tell,
and I was never one to talk about people's
nasty habits.
But it all comes out in the wash.
Thank God for cleansing and forgiveness.

Funny how I end up in this place,
White and Colored
like we been best friends all our lives.
I guess some things do change.

"Did you bring me any thing to eat?"
I produce a package of hard mint candy
"You remembered," she smiles.
          "I'll eat two now and save the rest for later."
She asks me to rub her legs
once more before I go.

Woman at the Window

Alice had her looking glass. I had the front room
window to take me far from the reach
of what held me to the house of my growing,
held me tight to what was mine and what
could be mine beyond the glass, beyond
the mirror, beyond those days of wanting and
anger and hunger and never enough.

You tried but could not give what was needed,
what I couldn't name, what I didn't know,
what I couldn't see, but knew was there.
If I just looked hard enough or long enough,
or had the patience.

I look at me then—angled, thin, no signs of laughter.
This must have been before the
recognition. This must have been the self to whom I
promised to never look back,
standing in a place I would never return.

The Lives Within Me

I become my other selves,
speak the language,
wear clothes of Bantu.
The Zambezi valley
is cooler than the Amazon river village
where I died giving birth.
My body tastes like guavas
that cover the ground above my grave.

In many skins, I have lived,
my faces stare not in mirrors, our image
reflected in a current lover's eyes
or in water of a still salina.
These spirits speak to me at night
through the cries of my born
and unborn children,
I listen, offer lullaby.
one by one they leave me,
claimed by the serene, like shadow
put to shadow.

I become a catamount
hunched in a cool mountain cave.
When human again, I find perfect
memory of a place
where a circle of elders watch the birth,
my mother's screams on my breath rejoice

because I am born
a male child this time,
a warrior, straight-legged, well-rounded head
the elders approve.
Teach him the father's way, they say,
one day he'll speak through ancient tongues.

Such a long memory knows to laugh
at Egyptian hieroglyphics,
memory clarifies histories,
has whispered many secrets.

Today the scent of eucalyptus,
a subtle stench,
almost hidden by the gay sport of children,
leads me to a rumbled ruin of rocks,
where I (the chosen princess for the water gods)
watched my young sister, sacrificed,
melted into the charred stones.
Her death made these sweet blossoms bleed.

These selves are manifested
like strands of silvered hair at the temples
around the face's edge,
they stare back, defiant, reluctant,
almost scared, they be, they become me.
They do not mind my daily rituals of waking
and sleeping, this ordinary living.

These selves
do not interfere or talk out of turn.
They come, they come
to me like rain,
a beating on windows,
and push me beyond
dreams into consciousness.

Robert Ray Jones Jr.

When she sees him put on his cap,
the brim dipping over his left eye,
Faith is surprised
at how much he looks like his father.
He has his walk too.
Same bow-legged gate, and he's starting to
wear out his shoes.
So yesterday when her eight-year-old son
asked to be called by his real name,
same name as his father,
who sees him on alternate holidays,
a year since she's let him go alone,
she tried to smile away her alarm.

Was there ever a time to tell him
of the bedroom door off its hinges
for weeks the year he was born?
Or how his father kept it there, a reminder of
what happens
if she kept any more cash stashed, if she hid
any more cookie jar secrets?
Or how his father said he didn't want to hurt
her and promised never to take that shiny kitchen
cleaver anywhere near her sweet dark body.
He said the splintered hole in the wood door
was a joke.

So when she asked, where was he going
and before she could recant her words,

she felt his answer.
"There you go, bitch, trying to get in my
business."

She couldn't tell her son that when
he frowned his face after her reprimands,
she sees the same anger that forced her
to jump from the second story window
with him, a six-month-old baby, in her arms
and that she had run two blocks before
noticing the swell of her broken ankle.

Family Portrait:
The Affirmation of Virginia

You wouldn't have known her
infant-girl-sister
in your mother's arms. She was dead
long before your arrival. Her small existence
marked only by the moments it took
these images to hold to paper. But there you
are centered among them— your hair
a youthful cascade around your shoulders,
smiling, your wish fulfilled,
the family portrait completed.
Only time and lost memory will destroy this proof
since you no longer speak the intimate
language of love with the living, your silence,
like a prayer, is what holds you to them.

While You Are Waiting

Sing softly, and gently sway at midnight
To calm the inside restlessness
Whisper mothering words to surround the
Swell of the one unborn
Read quietly
The rituals of trust and concern for the ears
Of the young ones
You nurture
Call loud their names
Then feed their spirits with the hums and
Hugs of a touch
That you remember once rocked you to sleep

Tell again the peace you felt
That first moment you knew of the coming
Of this new life
This will be the story that will
Be carried in the silence of dreams
Forever in the laughter of tomorrows.

Resolving Distractions

I sit for long moments
and watch the ripple beneath my roundness
reassured by the rumbling inside.

I marvel at this fullness,
as if I were the first
to discover the clamor of the unborn.
I think of my mother
and her mother, who had by my age
fourteen births between them—
confirmations of their reason to be.

The women will take me to the birthing room,
prepare my place, make ready the
cooling cloth,
keep tepid the welcome water,
tell me when to push and breathe,
when to wait, scream,
when to push and breathe.

Water Walker

For Sankara

This new crawler has made a catch-can game
and dares to test my hand.
He measures my quickness.
Will she come?
He laughs and heads face first for the floor.

When he gets to edges, he keeps going.
Like the water walker, he has no fear of falling,
some God-guided hand pulls him back.

But I am like Peter,
who even after a day of feeding multitudes
their fish and bread,
thought it an apparition
when the Man walked on water.
Only when the wind stopped
did he believe.
I, too, had replaced trust with doubt.
Still I know my limits in sky and deep water.

The Griot Comes to America

Jali man with your Kora of calabash and skin,
speak to me, daughter of son of son
of Mandinka that I am.
Echo in my ears has grown strange
to the voice that sings my histories,
that would laugh and say,
she has forgotten her place
beside the one who makes music.

Seriously Now, I Wanted to Run

The new girl's little sister
had no fingers on her right hand.
She was born with an unopened fist,
had three operations
to force a thumb from the pudge of flesh
so she could plait her own hair.

At the Bible School's
summer celebration,
she pushed palm into mine,
her smile stopped my pull away.
We completed the circle of hands.

In the Old Neighborhood

All the kids called her Chunky.
Even her own sisters would taunt
the big, dark, black girl.
She would run home crying,
her coat, always missing buttons,
flapping open,
her dress never long enough
to cover her ashy, scarred knees.
Someone said she had no father.

Once a year, our Sunday school class
collected money for the poor.
When the time came,
they picked me to place
the fat Christmas turkey
at their door.

Street Story

We was just having fun
and my boy, Jeeter, happened to have
a gun in his pocket. He wasn't trying to hurt nobody
the gun was just for show he said.
But then this dude
came walking up the street,
we knew he wasn't from around here
his colors was all wrong.

Bang, bang, you're dead, Jeeter said,
and before we knew it
the dude was on the ground
a hole in the middle of his face.
I ain't never seen nothing like that before
he didn't have time to cry
he was just bleeding all over the place.
I couldn't run and then one of my boys just
pulled me away
we left him in the street, we just left him,
hole in the middle of his face.
His silence screams at me nightly.
Jeeter says he didn't mean nothing, the dude
just got in his way.

Hold Your Breath, Hold Your Purse
Close to Your Body,
and Never Sleep in a Place Like This

Away from the sleep corner,
away from the chunky woman with her three
sticky children,
away from the man with blood on his face,
I sit in the safe section of the bus terminal's
waiting area.
I try to read a book,
try to find another place to be.
But the smell and cluttered noise
makes me part of this cataclysm,
part of the temporary forever
lived between places, the drop off points of
return and starting over.
I won't be here long is my only excuse
for being here at all.
A blue-suited woman with two-color eyes
smiles
her way into a conversation, she offers a mint
and drawls her speech,
"Down South is where I'm headed, the baby sister,
Rhonda May,
took a turn for the worse, she's the only
family that's left,
the bus takes so long,
she may die before I get there."

The blue-suited woman rolls her eyes toward
the direction of the smell,
a cop clears the corner, slow moving
men scatter.
"Ain't that ashamed," her talk now at the gray lady on her
right,
"grown men living in used bags."
I slip back into my book,
try to find another place to be.

Susquehanna Street Morning

Susquehanna Street
has the best pickings
and it is Solomon's Wednesday
morning stop.
A step to the left and he would have missed the shining
steel-head,
now retrieved from the sidewalk crack.
He slips the pin into a rubber-banded box
with his other pieces of silver,
places it on top of a grocery store cart filled
with bags—on bag of tin can tabs to sell as rings or barter
for bread loaves,
one bag for colored glass,
another for uncolored,
even a bag of bags.
a small cup of copper weighted the carts, left
front corner.

Five blocks later, he's bent
at a row of curb-side trash cans
awaiting the morning run.
He rummages, as if at a bargain basement
sale, keeps only the best,
then leaves with a low mumble
of how it takes all week to collect what used
to take a day,
and how the city's new garbage plan

may force him to find another way to fill his cart.
He offers a greeting to a woman
paused at a bus stop. She snubs away,
ignores his hat tip. A small child peers at him
from behind her mother's hold.
At early ages they're taught
to keep their distance.

Taking Back the Time

Outside, the distant clock tower beats
A faint applause. Another hour has come
And will go—measured in sand,
Constant like an untimed hum
Or moan, an old and empty sound that needs
No words, but still it calls to me, listen.
My response is selfish, my wish: be free
Of this distraction. Why is it that I have been
Victim of what I can't control?
I shall take night back, be my own time
Keeper and with these thoughts, I'm whole,
complete. The minutes rest has defined
My place and answer: to be apart yet remain
A part— the joy that spirits claim.

I Am Put Again Outside Myself

I am put again outside myself
A mist of wind like second skin surrounds
Me. Music's brought me close enough to tell
The difference between this crowded silence
        and no sound.
Come closer were the words you spoke, come here,
You whispered. I unfold from sleep and turn,
Trace my fingers across your morning beard.
We lie in moments cool, our day unconcerned
With least of all these crowds in night spots,
Loud, where I've come to take my mind
Away from the place you linger.
So I laugh, mingle, drink my wine,
Refuse to be alone, disguise my real intention,
Enjoy the music, forget the might have been.

Sending Love Letters

I'll read your letter at least three times before
I sit, pen in hand, and attempt to respond,
Making complete the cycle between us.
Unfolding thin sheets, I look first at how you greet me,
My Dearest,
And then at how you send me back into
myself, ink marks stop at the edge
of the page, Love Always . . . Love.
I smooth creases from pages and hold on to a
promise, this single proof of our existence.

The Need of Disappearance

I wanted to write until I became pure word
expression beyond the utterance of tongue,
or these marks on paper,
but that is not how it happened.
Yesterday afternoon, waiting for my car to be serviced,
gave me an
extended lunchtime stay at the Eat'n Park.
The murmur from surrounding booths
invaded my concentration
my hands still numb with cold,
the room-length window was no barrier
to winter's end still weeks away, outside patches of
        dormant shrub and dead
grasses browning through melting snow on the hill along
side the salt bleached road.

Was I trying too hard?
This was not even a pretty day,
sun muted behind shades of gray sky.

I wanted to write me back into being
back into life, word by word—
house, earth, shadow, fire—
each declaration sacred, celebrated,
each silence freed by its own circumstance.

Fallen Fruit

The soft spot
like the gray stoop,
like the forgetfulness,
like the brittle balance
one day she woke,
it was just there—blood stopped blue
just below skin—a new bruise
to hide in long sleeves.
They come more frequently,
an ottoman bump,
or how she tripped upstairs,
she tells the mirror not to do it again.
and promises to handle
this old fruit with gentleness,
its one way to preserve.

Waiting for Familiar

For a moment
I did not know the road
the dark had taken over where memory
stopped. But I kept driving,
waiting for familiar signs—bumps,
bends, curves—that would take me home.

For a moment
the night and the rain had misted
away, the safeness, all cognition
I thought I was lost
I thought
this must be how she felt
the day I found her in the middle of the
street, her hat hiding uncombed hair,
she wore her slip on the outside
of a floral-printed house dress,
one stocking, loosened from its knot below
her knee,
was bunched at her ankle.

She was on her way
somewhere
before she was stopped
lost
among familiar signs.

She looked at me
without perception,
as if I had the face of a stranger,
she backed away like a frightened child.
I took her hand,
Grandmother, let's go home.

Man, Woman, Children, House, Spirit, Garden, Love

1

Death strokes the bottoms of her feet.
Feet she keeps closer to the ground now,
a slow shuffle. In the middle of the night,
he lies awake and awaits her return to his bed.
Something cold rattles the house.
Her body needs rest,
but she can't get any sleep.
She's got things on her mind.
Gonna get her house in order,
find comfort in the kitchen.

2

One child for every day of the week,
ten years of her life
bleach-whiting diapers
and rubbing cracked, dried hands.
In her house, she has found no silent corners.

3

The house has never settled and is anxious to be heard.
The floor gives way to nervous secrets.
Years of age are showing
Skins of pain,
seven layers peeling,
color from color,
dark and slow death coming.

4

Love Jesus, Love Jesus, Love Jesus.
Be a lover of neighbors,
Love Jesus, Love Jesus, Love Jesus.

5

She does not like bitter greens,
Always picks collards after first frost.

6

"Every wise woman builds her house
but the foolish pulls it down with her hands."

7

She said she'll love him even in death.
He said he's not afraid.

Book Learning

When my great Aunt Lizzy
was eighteen and colored,
her first paying job was cleaning toilets
in a store that wouldn't allow
her to come through the front door.
If she had a book then
she says she wouldn't read it
"cause they be writing books
for the wrong people."

Measure of Distance

I've come back to right her life in my mind,
to find who lives in studied darkness, to find the woman

who wrote a birth, wrote a dying.
she survived a killing death.
Her wounded womb rests,
now past prime giving time.

Not a day goes by when she's not reminded
there were choices to be made.

Conversations carry us back and forth
between our separate memories.

Oven warmth, hearth fires, do not play with fire or stones
warming fingers, child too close to flames, too young for
terror

the scream an eternal burning, thigh-length scar grew as
she grew
a stubborn reminder, oven fire,

coal heat, black dust, feed the open belly
furnace in the basement,
red glow sleep, wake to sturdy put of coffee
brewing, boiling water rumbles

Mother speaks.
Where have you been? Gone so long from
home. Stay now.

Daughter speaks.
I've been crammed in this corner of your living.

Mother speaks.
I do not complain.

Daughter speaks.
There was never enough time, never enough room.

Mother speaks.
Everyday is a warning.

Daughter speaks
There is no last word.

One Woman Talking

If I praise
or converse with those women's women,
would someone get confused,
think I was one?
If a woman is too long without a man,
the question comes up
but not to her face.
Her walk is watched for unfemale
signs . . . ah huh . . . see . . . she must be one
(a lesbian) words are whispered.

Some of my best friends are,
or thought about it or laughed and shied
away, afraid to confront too closely,
not wanting to be too curious.
They said, we don't want any confusion.
We love ourselves some good strong men,
have the scars to prove how much,
but we don't want no confusion.

No confusion in the teaching of woman talk
and the taking of woman time.
because all women are the same.
We have mothers with hot kitchen tricks,
secrets shared on visits home,
boil the water then add the beans
leaves lumps in batter,

be who you are daughter,
trust rice to steam.

We have fathers who wanted to be more
than enough, the prince, shining,
but now dull-eyed, losing hair,
preoccupied with simple conversation.
What are you going to be when you grown,
if you ain't going to be like me?

Would you deny that it's the girl-friend
who would come at any odd hour, who
would be discarded
for the love of a man, who would come
again to fill the need
confirm the belonging, praise the flesh, the
hair, the words,
who listens in the still, stayed house.

She would come breath-close and taste salt
her time not measured by inches or dollars
she would stay, gentle away with tea, talk
never laying a hand on hand, she would come.

But we don't want no confusion.

Today I saw two women, knee to knee,
no secret, the excitement of these lovers
they took steps beyond known limits,

lines crossed like bleeding colors,
splattered, uncontrolled into a blur
I turn away, quick and flushed, caught
somewhere between
understanding and confusion.
To each her own, to each the bond.
To many I am seen as just
one woman talking.

Sestina For Michael
Returning Home

We're guided past the white heaps, shadows
                    along the road:
snow fallen prey to the distortions of night.
Come morning, he will have a new place to sleep,
when we gather to say goodbye and sing his songs.
It is by instinct that we go to the house
to mourn in rooms where we played as children.

Death-talk was not discussed with children.
Our closest encounters were the trails of cars
                  up the road,
And the visit to the family house,
bringing food, preparing for the long night
wake; where elders chose the favorite song to sing,
comforted the Mother, who found no solace in sleep.

His Mother always had to remind him to sleep,
the youngest of her three children,
the one with the voice. He would sing
in the choir of the Baptist church up the road.
She'd sometimes find him awake at night
thinking of his music. She knew he'd not stay
                  long in her house.

Only a half a street of houses
remain, the others had fallen while we slept

in other cities for ten years, our first return tonight.
We come to share our outside lives and show our children
the places that open with memory as we follow the road,
calling us as sure as the voices that sing.

He found new friends with the songs he sang,
he'd go to his house
not alone, or sometimes they rode
away hours, avoiding sleep,
played with their lives like children
with toys—no regard for convention or night.

Nothing is ever the same, especially at night.
He lost his voice, lost his songs.
The mothers watch him with frantic eyes;
                    they keep their children
at safe distances from the house.
They watch from windows, while children sleep.
Such curiosities up the road.

This is the last night that we'll spend in this house,
it echoes with old singing. His Mother cries herself
                              to sleep,
he was the second of her children that she put in a box
                and followed down the road.

When Lugenie Frances Died

When Lugenie Frances died
the family knew no other way.
The wake was held the third evening:
women in the kitchen,
men on the front porch,
children in the backyard.
At the funeral, mourners lined even the back
          pews of the Mount Sinai
Missionary Baptist Church.
Mary Turner sang, "Precious Lord"
and let the spirit lead her and Lugenie's
seven sons
down the isle as they carried their mother's body
across the courtyard to the colored cemetery.
The youngest daughter followed
with a gladiola spray.
She now has the duty to come and spring
clean the grave.

Eating Watermelon

After the picking thump,
eating watermelon was an art
I had almost mastered
until I saw
in Yosti's dime store window—
a rolling-eyed, black faced figurine,
big red mouth as wide as the wedge
balance on its knees.
All the other children laughed
at the grinning horror
staring back at me,
so at age eight,
I freed myself of melons.

A few summers older,
on a trip down South
my conviction was challenged
when Grandma's neighbor, Brother Bailey
issued a whole melon to each child
at the street fair picnic.
He had shown no restraint as he proceeded
face first into his wedge of red.
He was not even slightly embarrassed as he
joined the boys
spitting seeds at the brindled cat under the table,
a circle of black remained after it stretched away
and found another place to shade.

But that grinning toothed memory
would not fade, it would not let me
celebrate the sharing of cool fruit.
I picked at the seeds, quietly ate my melon
a distant laughter, haunting.

And Miss Emma Waits

Every evening
Miss Emma wears her Sunday hat,
ready with lesson and song,
on her way to the junior mission meeting.
She is distracted by the night shift change
and is escorted back to her room
with her window, chair, and a place
to shelve her world.

Miss Emma says
she can not sleep
on sheets with edges, will not sleep
in a place without air.
She says, the night nurse watcher,
with her wide white,
she stole the air,
takes it away if I sleep
and she'll take my money too.
Miss Emma looks for her red coin purse,
still under her pillow and counts,
fifteen dollars and eight cents.
she refolds a two dollar bill, takes a breath,
puts it back.

Every midday Miss Emma and friends
are wheeled or wander into the sitting room
to wait for familiar bites of laughter,

and visitors who come
one by one
each with a promise to return.

Marshall's House of Hats

Marshall was the hat-man,
wore them to keep sun from his eyes,
except his summer panamas,
which he wore to impress the women,
had one on the day
he went to ask Ora if he could marry her,
although he didn't say nothing about taking
no train north away from Georgia.
That straw brim made him look prosperous and honest
so there she was in the middle of a hard city,
her house cluttered with his old hats.

Even that last morning,
he put on the plaid apple jack and went
outside, like an overseer, guarded the yard
from the back porch swing,
waved his cane to tell old Jim
the art of the tomato and red rose.

You could hardly tell
his head was shrinking along with his body
after that second stroke.
If she padded the inside seams with tissue,
you could hardly tell.

The First Word Said Was Nowilayme

1
In the middle of her prayers
she stopped,
not wanting to die in sleep.

2
I am always cold.
In the night my fingers and half my feet stiffen.
I do not think it is death beneath my bones.
I think death comes with a warm running,
a loose haired touch welcomed on a bare back.

3
Understand the meaning of prayer
before you teach your children.

Birth Markings

"Each child must pass from womb-warmth through hands
of fire before it can claim spirit."

The woman opens the contracted fist,
tiny fingers grasp air
then close again.
The sign, this child should be among the living,
a small mark of his birth marring his palm;
touched by the ink of God,
a blessing to its mother.

Imani's third child was wrong-way born
and tried to cut its own path into being.
It died before the
soul settled and steadied its breath.
She does not mourn its dying;
child of devil and wolves
must be set beyond the bush
or eaten by its mother's mouth.

Meaning of Life

Struggle, tomorrow, in time, sleep
I want more from this world, ordinary boundaries
The gift, morning, air, amen,
touch, woman on a corner, revolution, beating
of drums, attitude, children at play, dead end streets
the task of living, oneness, speak of the elders gone
from home, know thy self, alone, determined
walk in the winter woods
universe, work, in his house, I'm tired, rest
I have been here once before
In the middle of the night I wake up alone
the last word was the first word repeated
and repeated
how can you have both
from whose eyes have you taken that story
lust, solitude, a good book
remember the starving children of the world
six hours in a birthing room focus and push
the struggle of new life
small fingers grasping at air
frustration

Awake at Midnight

He always falls to sleep
first and I am left to find faces
in ceiling cracks or connect flowers on sheets.

I move the tangled heap
of covers with a still half hour to waste.
He always falls to sleep

before the conversations ends, my tongue to keep silent.
So instead of sheep I calculate on ceiling cracks or counts
flowers on sheets,

pink rose, blue bud, then green
stem, like fresh flowers left untamed, they always fall.
He's too asleep

to notice the glass of water for which I've reached
on top of the passed-down bureau; old, faded,
sealed cracks connected or the flowers on sheets

of paper I pull from the drawer. I write to ease
the restlessness that is with me in this place
always. But tonight again I'll fall to sleep
counting ceiling cracks or connecting flowers on sheets.

Baking Bread

Bread baking is my way back into myself
and then out again
the steady knead
heal palm lift and gentle thrust
flour dust on sleeves and usually in my hair
sometimes I can almost feel my mother's eyes
watching over my shoulder, her hands guiding my hands
into the soft mound on the kitchen table

Momma taught all of her children how to knead dough
she would coat her fingers and
pastry cloth with an even layer of white
her hands moved with ease
the ritual had begun and ended with the second rising
of oven ready bread
a warmth worth the wait

Bread bakers are
the food givers

For a woman
to share her food is to share her wealth
abuse her table and abuse her as well
food is strength, it is power,
it is history passed down like an heirloom treasure
it is lineage, a continuance
passed on like a name

Learn to bake bread
and you learn the lessons
of patience, of persistence, and discipline

Learn to bake bread
and you will know the elements
needed for a strong mind's growth,
for nation building
and for love.

Until the Telephone News of Death Was Sent by Drum on Wind

Whether you cry or not
he died, is dead,
your seventy-five year old father
and you did not know
until one month later
and crying is not now in you.

He's already ground-deep and placed
under the blue gum trees
on the far edge of the farm
that confirmed the boundaries of his land.
He taught you the process of corn,
from earth to mill to table.
5,000 miles away,
you put corn in your garden
as a way to keep close to the sun
that warmed his back
and watched him stiffen with age.
You ask of this warmth,
where was the message,
where was the voice that called his sons home?
How will you forgive them,
those who kept you away from your father's dying?
You, who planned to be home soon,
in another country for so long

Closet Cleaning

This is necessary. This is vital
clarity, purpose rendered in the cries
that pull me from sleep
give comfort and start the business of day
then it comes
bone knowledge, an unexpected prevision
It was never about me. Was it?
Those battles of flesh and spirit
from the very beginning until now, in this house
except for the known one
no one really leaves this place with enough said.

How long did it take for me to be
comfortable in my own stare.
My face, showing
age, adjustment
in the mirror
looking like my family's history
if I didn't know
me—the unconcealed blotches
the gaps between my teeth
the hair that I pluck from my chin
would I know me broken in glass,
relaxed around the creases.

On the outside edge of my own agenda
penciled in at three o'clock
between the pruning of roses
and the car care grooming
the apparent appearance of importance and priorities
counting the done and left to be done
like Abram before the naming counting stars to number
        descendants
        limited by my eyes seeing
to trust is not to chance
when the answers come
you will know the questions.

Silence

I couldn't tell you how it actually felt to live with a thing
that hovers, that surrounds, that becomes us and without
knowing it, we came to welcome the wait, the silence, and
so much empty space between us and the world outside. I
couldn't tell you because what you would find horrible,
for us didn't have a name. No comfort for a child's night
dreams of terror—awakened by unceasing screams from
the room, how we would sit, three sisters, a refuge unto
ourselves, and watch for signs, movement from behind the
door. I think I remember a time when she did come,
when she did comfort our growing, when she said I will
always be, a time when she didn't stay closed in her room,
emerging before the dinner hour, she put on the leg that
gave her balance enough to prepare the meals and the leg
was the least of her worries, its wooden stiffness remains a
constant while her own soft flesh sloughed away. Slowly
inside and out she was leaving us. I couldn't tell you that
there were days that I prayed she would go and nights I
hoped for her once again wholeness or the steady hand's
ritual brushing of hair, and the hum from a voice that
would sing me to sleep.

Salvation

Preacher man, Preacher woman,
You know us in this moment.
Our stories used to urge the right way in,
ease the wrong way out.
If we don't listen now
this time it might be too late—
> no promise of tomorrow.
You lift your hands to— "commit them into your hands,
Lord."
> Admit the human same that you are as we
> but not as lost, not as helpless.
Sobering words
not your own you say,
Hear me, hear Our Father-Mother-Maker,
and we be water-warned,
no longer weary, wild, or wayward.

Ceremonies in Blood

For years she tried to keep her blood blue
until the day she woke up dead.
Menarche, the first blood,
her last morning.
Women fill the house with whispers.
It's time to tell her
she can not be touched;
she must have a room away from the others,
gather her things, burn old sheets and clothing.
Tell her she is to welcome the secret
ceremonies of blood.
She rocks in the cradle of hands.
Tell her to keep away from the men
and the man-myths.
If she thought she was dying,
if she woke up dead,
a woman wouldn't tell such stories.
Man said, Keep her silent,
away from the water
to stay clear of her,
stay out of her sheets,
wait for the cleansing.

And the women said,
Tell her the power of springs,
show her you have no scars,
no open wounds.
Tell her the truth,
not to fear the blood,
not to mourn its absence.

Poem Written When the Bathroom Ceiling Fell
Five Minutes After I Bathed my Infant Son

I was never that woman,
daughter of the poor,
loud in the heat streets,
never once caught in the corner of some dark
building of curses and unkept children.
We grew up—on the outskirts of integration—
and such women's lives were in documentaries
shown to reserve the movement.

My first after-college job,
at the neighborhood center,
now my chance to help her overcome
her bare bulb existence.
Maybe I thought if
I let her in my poems,
that would be enough.
But then I had this dream...

Hot flashes
too hot too loud
its too close too close
I could hear a baby's screams
I know I would not look
just for a second I would not look
until I got used to the blood then
I would stop my own screams

pray for some savior
I didn't know that one so little
could spill so much blood

I became her and was helpless.

Nothing is as Usual
(for Wesley David Mitchell, 1923-1999)

The first morning must be the hardest
The wake up call and morning coffee or tea
Breakfast warmed and waiting.

But the empty chair
pushed in at the table
old wood and worn
Just before the break of winter
Just before the last fall flora fades to brown
he would have liked this morning
A fresh crisp, sun-warmed start to finish the undone
Can wait for yet another day.

The first morning must be the hardest
With rooms of conversations still speaking
his voice or wearing his scent
On hats hung in wait of wearing
Neatly folded scarves, nearly never-worn
      wools and cardigans
Learning now how to hold a reflection in the mind-mirror
How to keep it humming a favorite tune
The music of his hello, listen for the still sweet
Slow message of morning mist and memory.

The first morning must be the hardest
Hands he held hold hands he held, holding hands,
embrace the alone left
Not lonely left
How do you prepare for so much in between
The hours of tomorrow and sleep again comfort?
Caring, keep them close.
Close your eyes and see him smiling
Again in the morning.

Crying for the Dead

I would cry for you: Randi Alexander, age five;
Kenya McPherson, eighteen months; Valerie Christian,
age twenty-one. I would cry for the twenty-eight name-
less protestors who marched to their death in a black
South African homeland and for the Brown woman and
her unborn baby girl who were part of a crowd
that was spayed with maddening gunshots and terror.
But who needs the foolish tears of a grown
woman crying into a heap of already-yesterday's news.

My own dead might bring cause for tears:
an expected grieving wail, loud and unencumbered,
let it out, child, let it out, cleanse your sorrows in a river
of tears.
But for the everyday dead
there is no time for crying.
Tomorrow the names will be replaced with a new list,
the next day with yet another, and it will go on like that.
It has always been like that.

Is is wrong that words of comfort are bought and sold as
a commodity in an untapped market?
How else cold those of us left living forgive ourselves for
the unasked prayers, for the unspoken words of praise?
We trade our silence for tears
and hope to reclaim the world's lost vision.

Sometimes There are no Words

She wanted her two dead-born babies
to live again inside her tired womb,
This time she would keep them safe, hold
them until birth, let them push their way to breath.

This time she wanted it: the rounding of a protruding
belly,
the fullness of breast,
the tender swell of nipple, those nauseous early mornings,
frequent trips to the bathroom, her ice-chip cravings.

She wanted no reminders, no pity, no explanations
She wanted no *God's will be done* to console her soul,
fill the space left open.

She wanted it,
not too late, not too early,
Her two dead-born baby boys.

Gave names of the living
so they might return,
so she might not forget
that after twenty-one weeks
they had reached their limit,
let go.

The Love Will Start With A
Word About Children

We celebrate their being, their possibilities
We celebrate a world created new through
the unvarnished eyes of children, their found vision
makes whole the fragments of songs, of books, of histories
that tell them why they should remember

songs mark the rhythm
dance to dance
foot to foot
of generations past

tongue spoken words of the first story
of the first people
in a place, a continent that gave birth to a thousand
nations

We celebrate the mother-told
and father-passed-down answers
to whose child are you

know where you come from
know which turn in the river will lead you home to your
beginnings
or the story of your beginning
and all over again

we will tell it to our children
and they will send it back to us
in the heart beat of tomorrow

Living through the Storm

We are losing her. Every day it becomes harder
and harder to bring her back into herself,
harder to keep her on this side of no confusion.
Everyday now complacency comes without struggle.

She seeks asylum from haunts of her own being,
Her refuge, in corners of upstairs rooms or
in any place, a reminder of what once was.

It starts with the hands:
they grown loose-fleshed and awkward,
she must hide them or keep them busy.
No one must know.
She must keep them busy.
So for hours, she scrubs bathroom
sink, tub, walls, and floor or plays cat-games with thread
and needle.
Then it's her head or feet.
She'll stand before a mirror and carefully
examine her face for changes, for glimpses
of a former self, now altered from age.

She no longer trusts morning to pull her out of a fog of
sleep, maybe tomorrow she'll be afraid to leave her bed or
she'll shy away from food, assume it's poisoned and say
that she's not hungry any way.

Sometimes her defiance is a total deflection from
the rock-solid woman who lifted the world higher.
No one can tell us what to do.
so maybe we'll pretend that it's just a phase or a
postpartum depression that has finally set in only now
thirty years have passed since the birth of her last child.

The doctors say, it will get worse before it gets better.
This behavior is to be expected
after a stroke or near-death trauma like hers.

But all I know is that
we are losing her
and everyday it becomes harder and harder.

Artesian Lover

On your first try

you drained this rock of water,

and until you came,
I'd never been dry—
not a season without
rain or river water stored in quart jars that lined the eaves
of my attention.

Knew I'd be ready for drought

Pre-warned about
the draining nature of men,
I kept all parts protected
my private aquifer (the only well within miles),
my small breast, my thighs.

And though you offered
nothing that could be considered
fair exchange, you praised
my sweet water,
brought promise of other springs.

Sisters Know

Sisters know
without speaking
lacking the reasons for words.

Eyes tell
red redemption
     there once was a man and then he wasn't.
Lips tell
parched in bitterness
     sapid longings denied.
Breasts tell
suck sagged
     hungers she could not fill.
Hands tell
clenched, holding
     sister's secrets
     hiding hurts in crevices of fold arms.

Sister know
having lived a darkened universality
this elipitical song echoes
     echoes
     a tacit fear.
She become the nameless chatelaine
dutiful, submissive
the pat-praised
mildly forgotten within mothering matrixes

permitted to soften and purify
wean, wipe clean,
while her own sweat-stained face
reflects into the eyes of sisters.

Sisters know
the cry sounds
      having hushed her own in hunted delights of self,
      fast fingered, snapped satisfied perfection pursuits
      without coloring thought.
The simplicity of death,
the sanctification of birthing,
baptismal waters part,
she emerges
      innocent, renewed,
      secured within the encompassing arms of sisters.

Sisters know
of love, of giving and of giving
      wrapped warm, searching beyond the realm of self,
      a unification, life within life
      a man-woman completeness
          a completeness that sustains
          the strength of sisters.

I Don't Throw Things Away
But Perhaps One Day I Will

Maybe when we're gone
someone, looking for fabric or pieces of quilt,
will find these unfinished poems.
The words would have gathered the smell of
things cherished
like the book of poems
my father gave me
that summer before I was grown,
though close to thirty by some clock in distant meter.
The pages had the flavor of cedar
and polished leather that lingered on all of his things.

Once while shining his brass and boots,
he stopped to show me both sides of an old coin
given to him by his Father's Father.
This has value, he said and closed it back into
his green army trunk with a 1950 annual,
an unclasped strand of pearls
and his bits of fortune.

Whenever I open the book and find his scent,
I know why I have become a collector of words,
and music and stamps,
and cornered treasures.

Before We Speak

Before we say goodbye,
We must say hello
And welcome the moments of now
Coming this minute, this hour, this day.

Before we say it's over,
We must say begin
Again and again and remember.

Before we see darkness
We must see light
Of day's dawn glow in the distance
Rise above trees and city rooftops
The waking hours
And assurance of all right
Just once more.

Before we speak the final words
We must share knowledge of first word
That spoke worlds into existence
Like Mother prayers for each new child
Like Father strong arms holding.

Before we ask for answered prayers
We must know that all will be answered.
So we must speak thanks for this day,
For every tomorrow.